Birds that prey together
Stay together

By Lu &Matt

Buythisbook.shop

To the magnificent birds of prey,
whose fierce loyalty and
unwavering dedication to family
inspire us all.
And to one's own family,
the true nest for the enduring
love and support.

Birds that prey together
Stay together

By Lu &Matt

In a world of blue skies
and forests of green,
some incredible hunters
are there to be seen!
With sharp-hooked talons
and eyes that are bright,
the raptors are busy
from morning till night.
But here is a secret,
a marvelous thing:
They're stronger together,
the birds of the wing!
From packs that are hunting
to guards on a wall,
they know that being united
is best of all.

There are eagles and hawks
and falcons so fast,
and owls and vultures,
they're built for a blast!
But others are clever
and social and grand,
like emus and peacocks
that roam on the land.
From the raven's quiet teamwork
to a falcon's high chase,
partners and teams
are all over the place!
They know a great lesson,
it's simple and true:
When they prey together,
they stay together too!

In a towering tree
in the North American sky,
Bald Eagles reign
as the kings way up high.
They mate for life
in a nest big and grand,
raising their family
with love close at hand.
One watches the babies,
one swoops for a dish,
teamwork forever
is their favorite wish!

Most hawks hunt alone,
but not Jon and Sierra.
They hunt in the dust
of a desert like area!
Like wolves of the sky,
they work in a pack,
to launch a coordinated
rabbit attack!
One flushes it out,
one waits by the bush,
they give that poor rabbit
a big-falcon-push.
Cooperation makes them
as smart as can be,
the most efficient hunters
that you'll ever see!

The Peregrine Falcon
is the fastest in the skies.
Two hundred miles per hour
as he zooms past your eyes!
Mach and his partner,
a falcon named Swift,
have city skyscrapers
and cliffs as their gift.
When intruders come snooping,
they dive and they swoop,
defending their home
as a two-birdie group!
With aerial stunts
and a flip and a flick,
their teamwork is speedy
and ever so quick.

When the sun goes to sleep
and the stars start to light,
Bubbles and Wisp
are the stars of the night!
The fierce Horned Owls
chase snakes in the wood,
as partners they are kinder
than anyone should.
Even silent night-hunters,
so fierce and so bold,
need a helping wing-hand
in the dark and the cold!

The California Condor is rare,
it is true, William and Sora
have big jobs to do!
They don't hunt for food
that is jumpy and quick,
they look for carrion,
that is their trick.
They watch one another
from way up so high,
if Sora finds lunch,
William follows through sky!
By looking together
they survive and they thrive,
with scientists helping
to keep them alive.

Turkey Vultures are not fancy
and they do not have flair,
but Aura and Glid
have a nose for the air!
With a superpower sense
that is really quite grand,
they smell all the food
that is hidden on land.
When Aura starts circling,
she's giving the sign:
"Hey Glid, come on over!
The dinner is fine!"
They scavenge together
to keep the world clean,
the best little cleaners
one's ever seen!

In the woods of America,
the Peacock is found,
in a muster of friends
that all huddle around.
Roger's tail is a wonder,
a fan of bright blue,
to attract his friend Iris,
and protect her, too!
When a predator comes
with a "Grrr" or a "Snap,"
the group yells a warning
to avoid any trap.
Roger looks big,
fanning feathers so tall,
giving Iris a chance
to escape from it all!

In the Australian outback,
the Emu stays low,
Drom and Em have a flock
where the wild grasses grow.
You don't need to fly
to be brave and be strong,
Drom and the dads
help the chicks get along!
If a dingo comes sniffing
for emu-sized lunch,
they work as a team
and they act in a bunch.
With powerful legs
and a kick and a hop,
they make sure the dingo
comes to a stop!

Small birds like the Warblers,
Pip and friend Warb,
wear colorful feathers
(a very fine garb!).
They join mixed-up flocks
with hundreds of eyes,
to watch out for hawks
in the bright morning skies.
If Pip sees a cat,
he gives out a chirp,
before any predator
gives a big slurp!
They huddle for warmth
through the cold of the night,
small birds are much stronger
when they stay very tight!

The Ravens are geniuses,
Bran and his Ink,
they are clever and tricky
and like to go think!
They use twigs as tools
and they play lots of games,
cooperation is the best
of their many aims.
They might lead a wolf
to a snack on the ground,
so the wolf opens up
what the ravens have found!
Unity brings them
success in the sun,
staying together
is how it is done!

From the desert sands
to the mountain peaks,
the secrets of teamwork
are what we seek!
Whether hunting in packs
or a family of two,
there's always a helping wing
waiting for you.

The End.